MASTER DRAWINGS
19th AND 20th CENTURIES

MASTER DRAWINGS

FROM THE COLLECTION OF
THE BUDAPEST MUSEUM OF FINE ARTS
19th AND 20th CENTURIES

SELECTED AND INTRODUCED BY
DÉNES PATAKY

HARRY N. ABRAMS, INC., NEW YORK

LIBRARY OF CONGRESS CATALOG CARD NUMBER 59-8844
PUBLISHED IN THE UNITED STATES OF AMERICA BY HARRY N. ABRAMS, INC , AND
IN HUNGARY BY CORVINA, BUDAPEST. ALL RIGHTS RESERVED. THIS BOOK MAY BE SOLD
ONLY IN THE U.S.A., CANADA & SOUTH AMERICA.
PRINTED IN HUNGARY. BOUND IN THE NETHERLANDS

INTRODUCTION

Most of the modern, non-Hungarian drawings of the Budapest Museum of Fine Arts—the best speci-mens of which are presented in this volume—derive from the collection of Pál Majovszky, a generous friend of the arts and of the Museum.

It was as an official and, later, between 1913 and 1917, as head of the Art Department of the Ministry for Public Instruction, that Pál Majovszky (1871—1935) came into contact with the Museum. In 1911, he start-ed a collection of modern drawings with the declared intention of ultimately bequeathing it to the Museum of Fine Arts. His collection embraces European drawings of the nineteenth and the early twentieth century, most of them by French artists (more than half of them—136 out of a total of 259 sheets—are the works of French masters). His collecting was pursued with an unerring flair for quality, coupled with refined taste and unselfish devotion; he also profited from the advice of Simon Meller, the head of the Museum's department of prints and drawings. His activity was cut short by World War I, and subsequently he could not enrich his collection. His love of the arts then found an outlet in the fine arts magazine, *Magyar Művészet*, which he edited for ten years, from 1925 until the end of his life. Before his death, in 1935, true to his original idea, he donated his collected drawings to the Budapest Museum of Fine Arts.

Due to unpropitious circumstances, the Museum scarcely had the means for adding new drawings to Majovszky's collection, but together with the Museum's original stock, it gives a comprehensive survey of the development of this art, if not a complete one. The works of several masters, particularly of the early nineteenth century, such as Turner or Géricault, are lacking, and the collection does not go much beyond the beginning of the twentieth century. Since graphic art is more immediate than painting and sculpture, and reveals its character like handwriting, the collection illustrates the evolution of nineteenth century art in general, as well as the sources of new trends in the early twentieth century.

The drawings presented in this volume give us a bird's-eye view of one of the greatest periods in art history, comparable in significance only to the Renaissance. During this period pictorial vision reached that summit, known as Impressionism, which committed to canvas the visual aspect, the illusion of reality. It was the ultimate achievement of a quest that began with Giotto and the Franco-Flemish miniaturists, continued through the Renaissance, and gathered new force in the Baroque movement of the seventeenth century, and the Rococo of the eighteenth.

The art of the early nineteenth century was still under the influence of two parallel trends, Romanticism and Neoclassicism, which had originated in the previous century.

In England, Romanticism became dominant and, at the beginning of the century, British art, as a result of its profound absorption with nature, achieved heights which significantly affected the further development of European art. The atmospheric quality of the great English landscape artists, with their miraculous color filtered through a vibrant atmosphere, is represented in a splendid landscape by David Cox, which still bears the imprint of the eighteenth century; in Bonington's coastal scene in sepia wash; and in the same artist's wonderful watercolor representing an agitated sea with fluttering sails, alive with the freshness of a sharp wind and the salty smell of the waves.

After the middle of the century, English art abandoned realistic expression and adopted the mannerisms of the Pre-Raphaelite school, which at the end of the century gave birth to "Art Nouveau." The Pre-Raphaelite phase is represented by a fine portrait of Swinburne in profile, by Dante Gabriel Rossetti, and a study by Sir Edward Burne-Jones, outstanding in its purity of line.

In France, the picturesque Rococo style gave way to the aloof coolness of Classicism, and the first note in nineteenth century French art was sounded by the dominant, classicist Academy. The art of the Empire period is represented in this selection by a single pencil drawing by Jean-Auguste-Dominique Ingres, dated 1818, showing the Forum Romanum; the drawing itself is of minor significance, scarcely evoking anything of the pure, fresh beauty of Ingres's best drawings.

The rigid forms of Classicism were shattered by the dynamic impact of the Romantic school, which appeared on the scene in the first thirty years of the century, and blazed the trail for further development. The collection is rich in works of the greatest master of the Romantic school, Eugène Delacroix. The earliest among them, dated 1824, is a highly picturesque watercolor showing a white horse, rearing on its hind legs, beating the ground with its hoof, its body contorted in frantic terror caused by a flash of lightning in the dark, stormy sky. The type and movement of the horse are strikingly reminiscent of the bronze figure of a horse by Leonardo, also in the Museum of Fine Arts. Other outstanding drawings by the same master are the pencil sketch for the 1828 lithograph of a tiger mauling a horse; a view of Tangier, recording an incident of the artist's African tour in 1832; illustrations for Hamlet; a pencil sketch for the plate lithographed in 1843 (which is better than the lithograph proper); and a pen drawing of St. Sebastian, a veritable gem which bears comparison with the works of the greatest old masters.

Following the works of this greatest of the Romantic painters come the extraordinarily picturesque and richly imaginative brush drawings, with their dominant black-and-white contrasts, by the leader of Romantic literature, Victor Hugo. The specimens in the collection were given by the illustrious author to Colonel Count Sándor Teleki who, after the defeat of the Hungarian struggle for independence in 1848—49, lived in exile. The most significant among them is a drawing protesting against capital punishment, made in 1854 in connection with the execution of one John Charles Tapner, a murderer. Five years later, when Victor Hugo raised his voice against the execution of John Brown, the crusader against Negro slavery in Virginia, he made several copies of the drawing, one of which he even had reproduced in mezzotint by his son-in-law, Paul Chenay.

The graphic artist par excellence of the Romantic school was Gustave Doré. The value of the Dante illustration reproduced in this volume is enhanced by the dedication to Franz Liszt.

Under the liberating influence of Romanticism and impelled, in many respects, by the English landscape artists (primarily by Bonington), the line of advance was mapped out by the Barbizon painters. Their art is represented by a fine pen drawing by Diaz de la Peña; a watercolor and a fine pen drawing by Théodore Rousseau; a picturesque chalk by Charles-François Daubigny; and a number of drawings by the greatest masters of the school: Camille Corot and Jean-François Millet.

Corot's sketches of the Colosseum, dated 1826, reflect the realism of his early works—more exquisite, perhaps, than his later style. A masterpiece of his late, poetic style is the drawing, *Shepherd with a Goat* (also used for a *cliché-verre*). Behind the linear design, the background shimmers in the silvery mist familiar to us from his late paintings.

6

The first of the Millet drawings reproduced here is a hill landscape in pen and watercolor. Next comes *The Cousin Farm at Gréville*, made in 1854 in the same manner as the first drawing. It is one of the finest examples of his style, partaking of the forcefulness of Rembrandt. His chalk drawings *Maternal Duties*, a sketch for the painting in the Louvre, and the *Woman at the Churn*, invoke the spirit of his paintings by their intimate, frank, natural tenor and bold, picturesque quality.

Honoré Daumier, whose art is in many respects akin to Millet's, is represented by two studies of heads in caricature (realistic topics often penetrated into art by way of caricature, just as they seeped through into the realm of literature via the picaresque novel). In addition, there are two veritable masterpieces by Daumier in the collection. The first is a sketch for the watercolor *Circus Parade*, in the Louvre; its tangled, tentative lines let the tragic undertone of the great humorist's art break through. The second is a charcoal sketch of Archimedes the scientist, poring over his circles, heroically oblivious of the warfare around him. In boldness of volume and movement, it rivals the expressive power, whetted on caricature, of the master's paintings.

This giant overshadows the rest of the graphic artists of his period. Even the delicate craftsmanship of a sketch by Paul Gavarni appears pallid, compared to Daumier's creations. Among the work of his contemporaries, only the art of Constantin Guys has preserved its freshness, thanks to his piquant brushwork that points toward Impressionism, his elegant forms, and ethereal tones. Noteworthy among his works in the Museum's possession are: *On the Champs Elysées, Women of Algiers* and *Grisette*.

Realism, which continued the trend of the Barbizon school, is represented in this selection by a minor drawing by Gustave Courbet, depicting the source of the Loue. Another example of this trend is a large-size, meticulous watercolor, *A View of Paris*, dated 1872, by Henri-Joseph Harpignies, whose style was a blend of the Barbizon and Realist schools. A watercolor sketch influenced by Impressionism, from the late period of the same artist, rounds out the survey of this movement.

The art of Henri Fantin-Latour, who strayed from Realism to a perverted form of naturalism—a "photographic" copying of the external world—is represented by a fine self-portrait in chalk.

Among the sculptors of this period, Jean-Baptiste Carpeaux contributes several sketches to the collection. The most outstanding among them, an excellent chalk drawing on the stationery of the French G.H.Q. in 1870, shows French troops marching through a crowded street.

Two fine sheets by the Dutchman, Johan Barthold Jongkind, and an airy, grayish-blue seashore, ruffled by the breeze and bathed in cloud-diffused light, by Eugène Boudin, all point directly towards Impressionism.

The Impressionist artists who followed in Realism's wake presented the perfect optical illusion: the apparent image of things, in lieu of their consciously-known form. Our galaxy—complete save for Claude Monet—opens with Édouard Manet, whose drawings are imbued with the unfading magic of beauty and harmony. Our first sample of Manet's works, the *Spanish Dancers* (1862), dates back to his early so-called "Spanish" period. The next one is a large-size sketch for the lithograph *Barricade*. With realistic horror, it recalls the Paris of 1871, yet at the same time raises this realism to the lofty heights of timeless, perfect art. On the verso is a study for the lithograph *The Execution of Emperor Maximilian of Mexico*, using in reverse—as if reflected in a mirror—that part of the composition on the recto showing the soldiers of the firing squad. The third and latest of his drawings, dated 1878, is a sketch of a motif occurring in several paintings. A highlight of Impressionism, it is an airy, fresh, India ink version of the Rue de Berne in a drizzle, bathed in the dull light of the rain's delicate gray tones.

The mainstay of the Impressionist section is represented by Camille Pissarro, with an India ink sketch of figures sitting on a bench; and Alfred Sisley, with three pastels—two fine sketches for the paintings *Early Snow in a French Village* and *The Church at Moret*, and a sheet of studies of geese.

Of the fourteen drawings by Auguste Renoir, one ranks among the finest sheets of the collection: it is a delicate, appealingly tender sketch, dated 1883, for his painting *Country Dance*, which captures the inexpressible sweetness of the moment. His drier style—almost a reversion to Ingres—of the middle of the 1880s, is represented by sheets of studies for the paintings *The Bathers* and *Battledore and Shuttlecock;* and a pencil sketchf of a seated woman. In the midst of these sharp, classicistic forms, his Impressionism partially reasserted itsel in the watercolor *Boating Party*, dated 1886, while his watercolor sketch for *The Bridge at Argenteuil* was entirely inspired by his rediscovery of Impressionism. A pictorial sketch for his *Music Lesson*, dated 1891, and a masterly chalk drawing of his late period, *After the Bath*, reflecting sensuous beauty and an unquenchable longing for youth, close the series of Renoir's selected drawings.

A sample of the art of Edgar Degas which replaced the illusion created with color by an illusion of fleeting movement—designed to impress the observer through its calculated casualness—is given in a chalk drawing of a dancer dressing, and a pastel study of a ballet dancer adjusting her bodice.

From the second generation of Impressionists, there are two almost caricature-like "snapshots" of Mlle. Marcelle Lender, and a scene at the Moulin Rouge, both splendid specimens typical of the refined, fastidious style of Henri de Toulouse-Lautrec, one of the great masters of modern draftsmanship and graphic art.

Another graphic artist of the period, Jean-Louis Forain, shows his little-known serious side in the plate *After the Vision*, whose tragic quality reminds one of Daumier.

The great Impressionist sculptor Auguste Rodin contributes a study sheet in India ink wash. A typical specimen of the sculptural sketch, it molds masses with the aid of light and shade. Other fleeting pencil sketches brushed over with watercolor are closer to Impressionist painting. His is the magic of expressing the human feelings playing beneath the surface of the passing moment, vibrant with light. This faculty is at its best in the chalk sketch for the portrait of Mme. Sévérine, one of the finest pieces of the collection.

Pointillism marking the disintegration of Impressionism, is represented by the remarkable sketch of a vagabond by Georges Seurat, and a typical watercolor by Paul Signac of a scene on the riverbank.

The style which succeeded Impressionism, although deriving from it, nevertheless ended by effacing its achievements; it branched off in several directions.

Paul Cézanne exploited every accomplishment of Impressionism, but consolidated the fleeting evanescence of the image into a logical correlation. His art, preoccupied with the problem of space and the structure of bodies, thus giving a foretaste of Cubism, is represented by two early pencil drawings: a study sheet, and a fine self-portrait; and by three watercolors from his later period, viz. a fruit still life, a landscape, and a plaster figure of Cupid, a motif which recurs in several of his works.

The paintings of the Dutchman, Vincent van Gogh, shifted from the portrayal of optical truth towards Expressionism as a result of his overcharged sensitivity and his heightened, passionate manner of painting. His early, gloomy period is represented by a charcoal drawing of a working woman. Next in the chronological scale comes the large pen drawing of *The Garden of Nuenen in Winter* wherein the framework of leafless branches and the hatched lines defining the space give the sketch a stern structural order. In the later pen drawing, dated 1888, picturing haystacks in a Provence landscape, the intensity of his exuberant colors—which in his paintings he enhanced by bold, dashing brush strokes—is rendered through the dynamic turbulence of his lines.

The third trend supplanting Impressionism, alongside Cézanne's emphasis on structure and Van Gogh's expressive art, was toward decorative art. It made its first appearance in the work of Pierre Puvis de Chavannes. It is represented in the collection by the sketch for a mural composition, among others.

The decorative style reached its climax in the works of Paul Gauguin. Two typical watercolors date from his Tahitian period.

8

The Fauves and the Nabis carried on the decorative heritage. The Nabis are represented in the collection by works by Pierre Bonnard, among which a portrait of the artist, the exquisite watercolor *The Yellow Lamp*, a gay sheet, and a splendid chalk drawing, *Toilette*, are the most remarkable.

Aristide Maillol, the sculptor, at first belonged to the Nabi group, and was a pioneer of the new sculptural style which took the place of the pictorial modeling of Impressionism. A sample of his art with its Mediterranean purity of form, is shown here in a particularly fine set of studies.

The chain of the development of French art in the gallery of the Museum of Fine Arts breaks off with a morbid, but beautiful, watercolor by Pablo Picasso, breathing the magic of a sawdust realm, the artificial world of the pantomime stage. It stems from his early period—perhaps the most artistic in the painter's career.

The trend of the arts in Austria and Germany diverged from those in western Europe and had no effect on their development. Classicism—with its offspring, Academism—and Romanticism were not irreconcilable opposites but appeared, ever since their beginning in the eighteenth century, in blends that varied according to the different periods.

Among the Museum's rich material from the early nineteenth century, middle-class "Biedermeyer"— a mixture of the Empire and Romantic styles—two great Viennese artists, Joseph Kriehuber and Rudolf von Alt are particularly outstanding. The brilliant watercolor portrait of Count Kajetán Erdődy's children by Kriehuber, and two views by von Alt of bygone Empire-style Budapest showing the National Museum and the old National Theater, have been included in this selection.

The large historic canvases of the dominant Romantic and Academic schools left their imprint on Germanic art of the second half of the century; only the academic works of Adolph Menzel, already approaching Realism, remained almost entirely unaffected. Among his many drawings in the collection, the most outstanding is a pencil sketch showing the interior of a church, dated 1883.

Even more brilliant are the works of Hans von Marées, with their Latin concept of form and their internal consistency of composition, unique in German art. His monumental art is represented by a beautiful study for his composition *Idylls*.

German Impressionism followed the French model—as was the case everywhere in Europe. It takes its place in the collection with the drawings by Max Liebermann, among which a self-portrait and a chalk portrait of Wilhelm von Bode, the eminent director of the Berlin Museum, are the best.

The last German artist to be included is Käthe Kollwitz, whose work reverts to the fundamental Expressionistic trend of the German spirit. The example presented here is a study for a lithographed poster depicting a proletarian woman. The profound social conviction that underlies her art is unmistakable here.

The Museum's collection traces the development of European art up to this point, preserving—even if fragmentarily—something of the magnificent artistic endeavors and beauty of the nineteenth and the early twentieth centuries, one of the greatest epochs in the history of European art.

LIST OF REPRODUCTIONS

The drawings were critically sifted for the first time in 1935 by Dr. Edit Hoffmann, head of the Department of Prints and Drawings of the Museum of Fine Arts from 1921 to 1945. The list of reproductions, while brought up to date by utilizing recent literature, is based on data taken from the manuscript catalogue compiled by her.

The drawings have often figured in exhibitions of the Department of Prints and Drawings of the Museum of Fine Arts in Budapest, for instance at the exhibitions of

— Modern Drawings in the Dr. Pál Majovszky Collection (1921),
— French Romanticists (1926),
— German Drawings (1932),
— French Drawings (1933),
— The Majovszky Collection (1935),
— The Finest Foreign Drawings of the Department of Prints and Drawings (1936),
— Modern French Drawings (1947, no catalogue),
— Daumier and His Contemporaries (1953), and
— The Best Drawings of the Museum (1956).

They were also exhibited in the former Ernst Museum at a showing of

— French Art in Hungarian Private Collections (1940).

The following abbreviation has been used:

MFA = Museum of Fine Arts (followed by the inventory number of the Museum).

D. P.

ENGLAND

1 COX, DAVID
(1783, Birmingham — 1859, Harborne)
LANDSCAPE WITH RETURNING HERD
Watercolor — $8^7/_8'' \times 11^7/_8''$
Esterházy Coll. — MFA 3081
Literature: Lázár, B.: Angol mesterek magyar gyűjteményekben [English Masters in Hungarian Collections]. "Magyar Művészet" [Hungarian Art], 1926, p. 197 (illustrated).

2 BONINGTON, RICHARD PARKES
(1801, Arnold — 1828, London)
COASTAL SCENE
Sepia wash — $5^5/_8'' \times 8^3/_8''$
Majovszky Coll. — MFA 1935—2626.

3 BONINGTON, RICHARD PARKES
BEFORE THE ENGLISH COAST
Watercolor — $5^5/_8'' \times 9^1/_8''$
Signed: "RPB. 1825"
Majovszky Coll. — MFA 1935—2627
Literature: Meller, S.: Handzeichnungen des XIX. Jahrhunderts aus der Sammlung P. v. Majovszky. "Die graphischen Künste", 1919, p. 29 (illustrated) — Lázár, B.: Angol mesterek magyar gyűjteményekben [English Masters in Hungarian Collections]. "Magyar Művészet" [Hungarian Art], 1926, p. 197 (illustrated) — Hoffmann, E.: A Majovszky gyűjtemény [Majovszky Collection]. "Európa", 1943, p. 150.

4 ROSSETTI, DANTE GABRIEL
(1828, London — 1882, Birchington-on-Sea)
PORTRAIT OF ALGERNON CHARLES SWINBURNE
Pencil — $10^5/_{16}'' \times 10^5/_{16}''$
Majovszky Coll. — MFA 1935—2640
Literature: Meller, S.: Handzeichnungen des XIX. Jahrhunderts aus der Sammlung P. v. Majovszky. "Die graphischen Künste", 1919, p. 30 (illustrated) — Lázár, B.: Angol mesterek magyar gyűjteményekben [English Masters in Hungarian Collections]. "Magyar Művészet" [Hungarian Art], 1926, p. 197 (illustrated) — Hoffmann, E.: A Majovszky gyűjtemény [Majovszky Collection]. "Európa", 1943, p. 151.

5 BURNE-JONES, SIR EDWARD
(1833, Birmingham — 1898, London)
STUDY FOR THE PAINTING "THE GOLDEN STAIRS"
IN THE TATE GALLERY, COMPLETED IN 1880.
Pencil — $7^1/_8'' \times 3^{11}/_{16}''$
Signed: "E B-J 1876 THE GOLDEN STAIRS"
Majovszky Coll. — MFA 1935—2631
Literature: Lázár, B.: Angol mesterek magyar gyűjteményekben [English Masters in Hungarian Collections]. "Magyar Művészet" [Hungarian Art], 1926, p. 203 (illustrated) — Hoffmann, E.: A Majovszky gyűjtemény [Majovszky Collection]. "Európa", 1943, p. 151.

FRANCE

6 INGRES, JEAN-AUGUSTE-DOMINIQUE
(1780, Montauban — 1867, Paris)
> THE FORUM ROMANUM
> Pencil and white body color — $5^{13}/_{16}$" × $12^{13}/_{16}$"
> Signed: "Ingres Rome 1818"
> Majovszky Coll. — MFA 1935—2725
> *Literature:* Rózsaffy, D.: Une exposition de dessins français du XVe au XXe siècle au Musée des Beaux-Arts de Budapest. "Le Bulletin de l'Art ancien et moderne", 1933, p. 282.

7 DELACROIX, EUGÈNE
(1798, Charanton-Saint-Maurice — 1863, Paris)
> HORSE FRIGHTENED BY A STORM. 1824.
> Watercolor and white body color — $9^{5}/_{16}$" × $12^{5}/_{8}$"
> Signed : "Eug Delacroix"
> Baron Schwiter Coll. — Cheramy Coll. — Kann Coll. — Bernheim Jeune Coll. — Majovszky Coll. —
> MFA 1935—2698
> *Literature:* Robaut, A.: L'oeuvre complet d'E. Delacroix. Paris, 1885, No. 101 (illustrated) — Exposition Delacroix. Paris, École des Beaux-Arts, 1885, No. 298 — Mauclaire, C.: E. Delacroix. Berlin, p. 52 (illustrated) — Roboussin, R.: Les animaux dans l'oeuvre d'Eugène Delacroix. "L'art et les artistes", 1914, p. 204 (illustrated) — Meier-Graefe, J. : E. Delacroix. Munich, p. 141 (illustrated) — Meller, S.: Handzeichnungen des XIX. Jahrhunderts aus der Sammlung P. v. Majovszky. "Die graphischen Künste", 1919 (illustrated) — Cézanne und seine Ahnen. Thirty-third publication of the Marées Gesellschaft, Munich, 1921 (illustrated) — Escholier, R. : Delacroix. Paris, 1926, Plate after page 102 — Exposition Delacroix. Paris, Louvre, 1930, No. 639 — Rózsaffy, D.: Une exposition de dessins français du XVe au XXe siècle au Musée des Beaux-Arts de Budapest. "Le Bulletin de l'Art ancien et moderne", 1933, p. 382 — Meller, S.: Majovszky Pál rajzgyűjteménye a Szépművészeti Múzeumban [P. Majovszky's Graphic Collection in the Museum of Fine Arts]. "Magyar Művészet" [Hungarian Art], 1935, p. 147 (illustrated) — Petrovich, E.: Egy eszményi magyar gyűjtő [An Ideal Hungarian Collector]. "Budapesti Szemle" [Review of Budapest], 1940, p. 205 — Hoffmann, E.: A Majovszky gyűjtemény [Majovszky Collection]. "Európa", 1943, p. 149 (illustrated) — Gyergyai, A.: Francia művészet a Szépművészeti Múzeumban [French Art in the Museum of Fine Arts]. "Budapest", 1947, p. 454 (illustrated) — Eugène Delacroix Zeichnungen, Aquarelle und Pastelle. Text von E. Delacroix, Ch. Baudelaire und H. Graber. Basel, Bruno Schwabe (undated), Plate 9.

8 DELACROIX, EUGÈNE
> TIGER MAULING A WILD HORSE. 1828.
> Pencil — $6^{1}/_{2}$" × $9^{3}/_{4}$"
> Study for the lithograph (Delteil 77)
> Marked with the stamp of the artist's estate
> Robaut Coll. — Majovszky Coll. — MFA 1935—2691
> *Literature:* Robaut, A.: L'oeuvre complet d'E. Delacroix. Paris, 1885, No. 287 (illustrated) — Meller, S.: Majovszky Pál rajzgyűjteménye a Szépművészeti Múzeumban [P. Majovszky's Graphic Collection in the Museum of Fine Arts]. "Magyar Művészet" [Hungarian Art], 1935, p. 138 (illustrated) — Hoffmann, E. : A Majovszky gyűjtemény [Majovszky Collection]. "Európa", 1943, p. 151.

9 DELACROIX, EUGÈNE
> THE WALLS OF TANGIER. 1832.
> Pen and sepia wash — $5^{13}/_{16}$" × $10^{3}/_{16}$"
> Marked with the stamp of the artist's estate
> Robaut Coll. — Majovszky Coll. — MFA 1935—2692
> *Literature:* Robaut, A.: L'oeuvre complet d'E. Delacroix. Paris, 1885, No. 422 (illustrated) — Meller, S.: Majovszky Pál rajzgyűjteménye a Szépművészeti Múzeumban [P. Majovszky's Graphic Collection in the Museum of Fine Arts]. "Magyar Művészet" [Hungarian Art], 1935, p. 138 (illustrated) — Hoffmann, E.: A Majovszky gyűjtemény [Majovszky Collection]. "Európa", 1943, p. 151.

10 DELACROIX, EUGÈNE
> HAMLET AND CLAUDIUS, *HAMLET*, ACT III, SCENE iii. 1843.
> Pencil — $10^{3}/_{4}$" × $7^{5}/_{16}$"
> Study for the lithograph (Delteil 110)
> Marked with the stamp of the artist's estate
> Donated by S. Meller — MFA 1927—2010
> *Literature:* Az Országos Magyar Szépművészeti Múzeum Évkönyvei [Annals of the Hungarian Museum of Fine Arts], V, 1929, p. 213, Fig. 14.

14

11 DELACROIX, EUGÈNE
ST. SEBASTIAN TENDED BY CHARITABLE WOMEN
Pen and bister wash — $10\,^{15}/_{16}'' \times 17\,^{5}/_{16}''$
This version of the subject, worked up in countless compositions since 1836, is the mirror-image of the painting dated 1859 (Robaut No. 1381)
Marked with the stamp of the artist's estate
Cheramy Coll. — Majovszky Coll. — MFA 1935—2697
Literature: Meller, S.: Handzeichnungen des XIX. Jahrhunderts aus der Sammlung P. v. Majovszky. "Die graphischen Künste", 1919, p. 1 (illustrated) — Cézanne und seine Ahnen. Thirty-third publication of the Marées Gesellschaft, Munich, 1921 (illustrated) — Meier-Graefe, J.: E. Delacroix. Munich, p. 27 (illustrated) — Rózsaffy, D.: Une exposition de dessins français du XVᵉ au XXᵉ siècle au Musée des Beaux-Arts de Budapest. "Le Bulletin de l'Art ancien et moderne", 1933, p. 381 (illustrated) — Hajós, E.: Francia rajzok kiállítása a Szépművészeti Múzeumban [Exposition of French Drawings in the Museum of Fine Arts]. "Magyar Művészet" [Hungarian Art], 1933, p. 326 (illustrated) — Hoffmann, E.: A Majovszky gyűjtemény [Majovszky Collection]. "Európa", 1943, p. 151 — Eugène Delacroix Zeichnungen, Aquarelle und Pastelle. Text von E. Delacroix, Ch. Baudelaire und H. Graber. Basel, Bruno Schwabe (undated), Plate 58.

12 HUGO, VICTOR
(1802, Besançon — 1885, Paris)
ECCE
Bister wash — $18'' \times 12\,^{3}/_{8}''$
The drawing was made in connection with the execution of John Charles Tapner, a robber and murderer, whose life Victor Hugo wanted to save by an appeal for mercy. Later, in 1859, he made several copies of the drawing on the occasion of the execution of John Brown, the abolitionist, and had one of the copies reprinted in mezzotint by Paul Chenay.
Signed: "Victor Hugo Jersey 1854"
Deposited in trust by the family of the Counts Teleki and Mrs. V. Domahidy — MFA 1913—402
Literature: Vikár, V.: V. Hugo rajzairól [An Essay on V. Hugo's Drawings]. "Magyar Művészet" [Hungarian Art], 1927, p. 268—271 (illustrated) — Rózsaffy, D.: Une exposition de dessins français du XVᵉ au XXᵉ siècle au Musée des Beaux-Arts de Budapest. "Le Bulletin de l'Art ancien et moderne", 1933, p. 382.

13 DORÉ, GUSTAVE
(1833, Strasbourg — 1883, Paris)
DANTE AND VIRGIL BEFORE THE GATE OF HELL
India ink wash, body white, and sepia — $16\,^{11}/_{16}'' \times 12\,^{5}/_{8}''$
Signed: "D'après la symphonie de l'abbé Liszt G. Doré"
Taken over from the National Museum, out of the estate of Franz Liszt — MFA 1905—1962
Literature: "Magyar Művészet" [Hungarian Art], 1933, p. 117 (illustrated)

14 DIAZ DE LA PEŇA, NARCISSE-VIRGILE
(1808, Bordeaux — 1876, Menton)
FOREST
Pen and ink — $3\,^{13}/_{16}'' \times 7''$
Marked with the stamp of the artist's estate
Majovszky Coll. — MFA 1935—2690.

15 ROUSSEAU, THÉODORE
(1812, Paris — 1867, Barbizon)
RIVER LANDSCAPE
(On the verso, a sketch of the same scene)
Pen and watercolor — $6\,^{9}/_{16}'' \times 6\,^{1}/_{4}''$
Marked with the stamp of the artist's estate
D. Malonyay Coll. — MFA 1917—439.

16 ROUSSEAU, THÉODORE
FOREST LANDSCAPE
Pen and bister — $4'' \times 6\,^{5}/_{16}''$
Marked with the stamp of the artist's estate
Majovszky Coll. — MFA 1935—2783.

17 DAUBIGNY, CHARLES-FRANÇOIS
(1817, Paris — 1878, Paris)
LANDSCAPE
Chalk — $11\,^{3}/_{4}'' \times 18\,^{1}/_{8}''$
Majovszky Coll. — MFA 1935—2684.

18 COROT, JEAN-BAPTISTE-CAMILLE
(1796, Paris — 1875, Paris)
SKETCHES FOR THE PAINTING OF THE COLOSSEUM
FROM VARIOUS ANGLES. 1826.
Pen and India ink wash — $11^7/_8'' \times 16^{15}/_{16}''$
Study for the painting in the Louvre dated 1826
Marked with the stamp of the artist's estate
Donated by F. Kleinberger — MFA 1911—229
Literature: Rózsaffy, D.: Une exposition de dessins français du XVe au XXe siècle au Musée des Beaux-Arts de Budapest. "Le Bulletin de l'Art ancien et moderne", 1933, p. 382—383.

19 COROT, JEAN-BAPTISTE-CAMILLE
LANDSCAPE
Charcoal — $9^3/_4'' \times 12^1/_2''$
Marked with the stamp of the artist's estate
Majovszky Coll. — MFA 1935—2680.

20 COROT, JEAN-BAPTISTE-CAMILLE
SHEPHERD WITH A GOAT. 1852.
Chalk and pencil — $12^1/_8'' \times 9^7/_{16}''$
In 1874, the composition was issued as a *cliché-verre* (Delteil 95)
Signed: "COROT"
C. Dutilleux Coll. — Robaut Coll. — Majovszky Coll. — MFA 1935—2681
Literature: Robaut, A.: L'oeuvre de Corot. Paris, 1905, IV, No. 2881 (illustrated) — Delteil, L.: Corot. Paris, 1910, No. 95 — Meller, S.: Handzeichnungen des XIX. Jahrhunderts aus der Sammlung P. v. Majovszky. "Die graphischen Künste", 1919, p. 10 (illustrated) — Cézanne und seine Ahnen. Thirty-third publication of the Marées Gesellschaft, Munich, 1921, Plate 4 — Rózsaffy, D.: Une exposition de dessins français du XVe au XXe siècle au Musée des Beaux-Arts de Budapest. "Le Bulletin de l'Art ancien et moderne", 1933, p. 383 — Meller, S.: Majovszky Pál rajzgyűjteménye a Szépművészeti Múzeumban [P. Majovszky's Graphic Collection in the Museum of Fine Arts]. "Magyar Művészet" [Hungarian Art], 1935, p. 140 (illustrated) — Hoffmann, E.: A Majovszky gyűjtemény [Majovszky Collection]. "Európa", 1943, p. 152 — Gyergyai, A.: Francia művészet a Szépművészeti Múzeumban [French Art in the Museum of Fine Arts]. "Budapest", 1947, p. 452 (illustrated).

21 MILLET, JEAN-FRANÇOIS
(1814, Gruchy — 1875, Barbizon)
HILL LANDSCAPE
Pencil, pen, and watercolor — $7^7/_{16}'' \times 9^1/_4''$
Marked with the stamp of the artist's estate
Majovszky Coll. — MFA 1935—2746
Literature: Meller, S.: Majovszky Pál rajzgyűjteménye a Szépművészeti Múzeumban [P. Majovszky's Graphic Collection in the Museum of Fine Arts]. "Magyar Művészet" [Hungarian Art], 1935, p. 150 (illustrated).

22 MILLET, JEAN-FRANÇOIS
THE COUSIN FARM AT GRÉVILLE. 1854.
Pen and watercolor — $8^7/_8'' \times 11^1/_8''$
The oil painting of the farm was made between 1854 and 1875
Marked with the stamp of the artist's estate
Majovszky Coll. — MFA 1935—2738
Literature: Meller, S.: Handzeichnungen des XIX. Jahrhunderts aus der Sammlung P. v. Majovszky. "Die graphischen Künste", 1919, p. 4 (illustrated) — Meller, S.: Majovszky Pál rajzgyűjteménye a Szépművészeti Múzeumban [P. Majovszky's Graphic Collection in the Museum of Fine Arts]. "Magyar Művészet" [Hungarian Art], 1935, p. 139 (illustrated) — Hoffmann, E.: A Majovszky gyűjtemény [Majovszky Collection]. "Európa", 1943, p. 152.

23 MILLET, JEAN-FRANÇOIS
MATERNAL DUTIES
Chalk — $11^{11}/_{16}'' \times 8^{15}/_{16}''$
Study for the canvas in the Louvre and the *cliché-verre* (Delteil 27)
Signed: "J. F. Millet"
Majovszky Coll. — MFA 1913—1515
Literature: Hajós, E.: Francia rajzok kiállítása a Szépművészeti Múzeumban [Exposition of French Drawings in the Museum of Fine Arts]. "Magyar Művészet" [Hungarian Art], 1933, p. 329 (illustrated).

24 MILLET, JEAN-FRANÇOIS
  WOMAN AT THE CHURN
  Chalk — 15⁵/₈″×9¹³/₁₆″
  Signed: "J. F. Millet"
  Majovszky Coll. — MFA 1935—2742
  Literature: Rózsaffy, D.: Une exposition de dessins français du XVᵉ au XXᵉ siècle au Musée des Beaux-
  Arts de Budapest. "Le Bulletin de l'Art ancien et moderne", 1933, p. 382 — Hoffmann, E.: A Majovszky
  gyűjtemény [Majovszky Collection]. "Európa", 1943, p. 152.

25 MILLET, JEAN-FRANÇOIS
  SEASIDE AT GRÉVILLE
  India ink, chalk, and white body color — 12¹/₂″×18¹¹/₁₆″
  Marked with the stamp of the artist's estate
  J. Dollfus Coll. — Majovszky Coll. — MFA 1935—2737
  Literature: Rózsaffy, D.: Une exposition de dessins français du XVᵉ au XXᵉ siècle au Musée des Beaux-
  Arts de Budapest. "Le Bulletin de l'Art ancien et moderne", 1933, p. 382.

26 DAUMIER, HONORÉ
 (1808, Marseille — 1879, Valmondois)
  STUDY OF A HEAD
  Indian ink, pen — 7¹/₂″×5¹/₂″
  Majovszky Coll. — MFA 1935—2687.

27 DAUMIER, HONORÉ
  STUDY OF TWO HEADS
  Bister, pen — 6¹/₄″×7¹/₈″
  Signed: "h. D."
  Majovszky Coll. — MFA 1935—2686
  Literature: Fuchs, E.: Der Maler Daumier. Munich, 1927, p. 211 (illustrated).

28 DAUMIER, HONORÉ
  ARCHIMEDES
  Charcoal — 16¹³/₁₆″×15⁵/₁₆″
  Roger Marx Coll. — Majovszky Coll. — MFA 1935—2685
  Literature: Meller, S.: Handzeichnungen des XIX. Jahrhunderts aus der Sammlung P. v. Majovszky.
  "Die graphischen Künste", 1919, p. 5 (illustrated) — Rózsaffy, D.: Une exposition de dessins français
  du XVᵉ au XXᵉ siècle au Musée des Beaux-Arts de Budapest. "Le Bulletin de l'Art ancien et moderne",
  1933, p. 383 — Meller, S.: Majovszky Pál rajzgyűjteménye a Szépművészeti Múzeumban [P. Majovszky's
  Graphic Collection in the Museum of Fine Arts]. "Magyar Művészet" [Hungarian Art], 1935, p. 142
  (illustrated) — Hoffmann, E.: A Majovszky gyűjtemény [Majovszky Collection]. "Európa", 1943, p.
  152 — Gyergyai, A.: Francia művészet a Szépművészeti Múzeumban [French Art in the Museum of Fine
  Arts]. "Budapest", 1947, p. 451 (illustrated).

29 DAUMIER, HONORÉ
  CIRCUS PARADE
  Red and black, India ink wash — 15⁵/₁₆″×12¹/₈″
  Sketch for the watercolor in the Louvre
  Signed: "h. D."
  Hatvany Coll. — MFA 1950—4276
  Literature: Hajós, E.: Francia rajzok kiállítása a Szépművészeti Múzeumban [Exposition of French Draw-
  ings in the Museum of Fine Arts]. "Magyar Művészet" [Hungarian Art], 1933, p. 325 (illustrated).

30 GAVARNI, PAUL
 (1804, Paris — 1866, Auteuil)
  MY HUSBAND!
  Pastel and white body color — 11³/₈″×8¹³/₁₆″
  Signed: "Gavarni Londres 49"
  Goncourt Coll. — Ch. Freund-Deschamps Coll. — Majovszky Coll. — MFA 1935—2717.

31 GUYS, CONSTANTIN
(1805, Vlissingen — 1892, Paris)
ON THE CHAMPS ELYSÉES
Watercolor — $8^5/_8'' \times 13''$
Majovszky Coll. — MFA 1935—2721
Literature: Hoffmann, E.: A Majovszky gyűjtemény [Majovszky Collection]. "Európa", 1943, p. 153.

32 GUYS, CONSTANTIN
WOMEN OF ALGIERS
Watercolor — $8^5/_{16}'' \times 12''$
Nadar Coll. — MFA 1916—141
Literature: Rózsaffy, D.: Une exposition de dessins français du XVe au XXe siècle au Musée des Beaux-Arts de Budapest. "Le Bulletin de l'Art ancien et moderne", 1933, p. 383 (illustrated).

33 GUYS, CONSTANTIN
GRISETTE
Watercolor — $15^5/_8'' \times 9^{11}/_{16}''$
Majovszky Coll. — MFA 1935—2723
Literature: Rózsaffy, D.: Une exposition de dessins français du XVe au XXe siècle au Musée des Beaux-Arts de Budapest. "Le Bulletin de l'Art ancien et moderne", 1933, p. 382 — Meller, S.: Majovszky Pál rajzgyűjteménye a Szépművészeti Múzeumban [P. Majovszky's Graphic Collection in the Museum of Fine Arts]. "Magyar Művészet" [Hungarian Art], 1935, p. 141 (illustrated) — Hoffmann, E.: A Majovszky gyűjtemény [Majovszky Collection]. "Európa", 1943, p. 153.

34 COURBET, GUSTAVE
(1819, Ornans — 1877, La Tour de Peilz)
THE SOURCE OF THE LOUE
Sepia, chalk and pencil — $15^1/_2'' \times 23^5/_8''$
Courbet sketched the scene several times between 1864 and 1872 (Hamburg, Kunsthalle)
Signed: "G. Courbet, La Source de la Loue"
Majovszky Coll. — MFA 1935—2682
Literature: Meller, S.: Handzeichnungen des XIX. Jahrhunderts aus der Sammlung P. v. Majovszky. "Die graphischen Künste", 1919, p. 6 (illustrated) — Meller, S.: Majovszky Pál rajzgyűjteménye a Szépművészeti Múzeumban [P. Majovszky's Graphic Collection in the Museum of Fine Arts]. "Magyar Művészet" [Hungarian Art], 1935, p. 146 (illustrated) — Hoffmann, E.: A Majovszky gyűjtemény [Majovszky Collection]. "Európa", 1943, p. 152.

35 HARPIGNIES, HENRI-JOSEPH
(1819, Valenciennes — 1916, Saint-Privé)
A VIEW OF PARIS
Watercolor — $20'' \times 27^1/_{16}''$
Signed: "Hy Harpignies. 1872."
Purchased in 1912 — MFA 1950—4291
Literature: Peregriny, J.: Az Országos Magyar Szépművészeti Múzeum állagai [The Possessions of the Museum of Fine Arts], III/2, p. 967.

36 HARPIGNIES, HENRI-JOSEPH
ON THE SHORE
Watercolor — $7^{13}/_{16}'' \times 10^3/_8''$
Signed: "Hy Harpignies 99"
MFA 1951—4436.

37 FANTIN-LATOUR, HENRI
(1836, Grenoble — 1904, Buré)
SELF-PORTRAIT. 1854—1856 (?)
Chalk — $11^5/_{16}'' \times 9^1/_4''$
A similar drawing is in the Albertina in Vienna
G. Régamey Coll. — Ch. Freund-Deschamps Coll. — Majovszky Coll. — MFA 1935—2702
Literature: Mme. Fantin-Latour: Catalogue de l'oeuvre complet de Fantin-Latour. Paris, 1911, No. 2292 — Meller, S.: Handzeichnungen des XIX. Jahrhunderts aus der Sammlung P. v. Majovszky. "Die graphischen Künste", 1919, p. 8—10 (illustrated).

38 BOUDIN, EUGÈNE
(1824, Honfleur — 1898, Paris)
ON THE BEACH
Pencil and watercolor — $5^1/_{16}'' \times 8^3/_{16}''$
Signed: "E. Boudin — 68"
Majovszky Coll. — MFA 1935—2664.

39 CARPEAUX, JEAN-BAPTISTE
(1827, Valenciennes — 1875, Courbevoie)
RIOTS IN THE STREETS OF PARIS. 1870.
Chalk — $10^7/_{16}'' \times 8^1/_8''$
On the stationery of the Quartier Général
Marked with the stamp of the artist's estate
Majovszky Coll. — MFA 1935—2672
Literature: Meller, S.: Handzeichnungen des XIX. Jahrhunderts aus der Sammlung P. v. Majovszky.
"Die graphischen Künste", 1919, p. 16 (illustrated) — Rózsaffy, D.: Une exposition de dessins français
du XVe au XXe siècle au Musée des Beaux-Arts de Budapest. "Le Bulletin de l'Art ancien et moderne",
1933, p. 383 — Hoffmann, E.: A Majovszky gyűjtemény [Majovszky Collection]. "Európa", 1943, p. 153.

40 MANET, ÉDOUARD
(1832, Paris — 1883, Paris)
SPANISH DANCERS
(Among them Lola de Valence and Camprubi)
Watercolor, India ink, pencil, heightened with body color — $9^1/_8'' \times 16^5/_{16}''$
Study for the painting in the Phillips Collection at Washington, D.C., made in 1862
Signed: "manet"
Ch. André Coll. — Majovszky Coll. — MFA 1925—1200
Literature: Meller, S.: Handzeichnungen des XIX. Jahrhunderts aus der Sammlung P. v. Majovszky.
"Die graphischen Künste", 1919, p. 10 (illustrated) — Glaser, C.: Manet. Munich, 1922 (illustrated) —
Az Országos Magyar Szépművészeti Múzeum Évkönyvei [Annals of the Museum of Fine Arts], V. 1929,
p. 211 (illustrated) — Hoffmann, E.: A Szépművészeti Múzeum új szerzeményei, II. Grafikai Művek [New
Acquisitions of the Museum of Fine Arts, II. Graphic Works]. "Magyar Művészet" [Hungarian Art],
1931, pp. 394—397 (illustrated) — Tabarant, A.: Manet. Paris, 1931, p. 519, No. 22 — Rózsaffy, D.: Une
exposition de dessins français du XVe au XXe siècle au Musée des Beaux-Arts de Budapest. "Le Bulletin
de l'Art ancien et moderne", 1933, p. 383 (illustrated) — Hoffmann, E.: A Majovszky gyűjtemény [Majov-
szky Collection]. "Európa", 1943, p. 151 (illustrated) — Tabarant, A.: Manet et ses oeuvres. Paris, 1947,
p. 52 (ill. p. 620, No. 557).

41 MANET, ÉDOUARD
BARRICADE. 1871.
India ink, watercolor on body white — $18^3/_{16}'' \times 12^{13}/_{16}''$
Study for the lithograph (Moreau-Nélaton 82)
J. Dollfus Coll. — Majovszky Coll. — MFA 1935—2734
Literature: Exposition du legs, en janvier 1884. Paris, École Nationale des Beaux-Arts, No. 119 — Exposi-
tion de l'atelier, en février 1884, No. 137 — E. Moreau-Nélaton: Manet. Paris, 1906, No. 82 — Meier-
Graefe, J.: E. Manet. Munich, p. 192 (illustrated) — Meller, S.: Handzeichnungen des XIX. Jahrhunderts
aus der Sammlung P. v. Majovszky. "Die graphischen Künste", 1919, p. 11 — Glaser, C.: E. Manet.
Munich, 1922 (illustrated) — Tabarant, A.: Manet. Paris, 1931, p. 530, No. 41 — Rózsaffy, D.: Une
exposition de dessins français du XVe au XXe siècle au Musée des Beaux-Arts de Budapest. "Le
Bulletin de l'Art ancien et moderne", 1933, p. 383 — Hajós, E.: Francia rajzok kiállítása a Szépművészeti
Múzeumban [Exposition of French Drawings in the Museum of Fine Arts]. "Magyar Művészet" [Hun-
garian Art], 1933, p. 330 (illustrated) — Hoffmann, E.: A Majovszky gyűjtemény [Majovszky Collection].
"Európa", 1943, p. 152 — Guérin, M.: L'oeuvre gravée de Manet. Paris, 1944, No. 76. (According to
this author, the drawing was, at the time, part of the Majorsky [sic] collection, although the latter had been
incorporated with the collection of the Museum of Fine Arts.) — Tabarant, A.: Manet et ses oeuvres.
Paris, 1947, p. 190 (ill. p. 620, No. 590) — Huyghe, R.: Le dessin français au XIXe siècle. Lausanne, 1956,
p. 83 (illustrated) — Martin, K.: Édouard Manet. Aquarelle und Pastelle. Basel, 1958, p. 13, Plate 10
(illustrated).

42 MANET, ÉDOUARD
THE EXECUTION OF EMPEROR MAXIMILIAN OF MEXICO
(On the verso of the drawing No. 41)
Study for the lithograph (Moreau-Nélaton 79).

43 MANET, ÉDOUARD
   THE RUE DE BERNE IN RAINY WEATHER. 1878.
   Pencil and India ink wash — $7^7/_{16}'' \times 14^3/_{16}''$
   Roger-Marx Coll. — Majovszky Coll. — MFA 1935—2735
   Literature: Meller, S.: Handzeichnungen des XIX. Jahrhunderts aus der Sammlung P. v. Majovszky.
   "Die graphischen Künste", 1919, p. 11 (illustrated) — Glaser, C.: E. Manet. Munich, 1922 (illustrated)
   — Tabarant, A.: Manet. Paris, 1931, pp. 545—546, No. 72 — Rózsaffy, D.: Une exposition de dessins
   français du XVᵉ au XXᵉ siècle au Musée des Beaux-Arts de Budapest. "Le Bulletin de l'Art ancien et mo-
   derne", 1933, p. 383 — Meller, S.: Majovszky Pál rajzgyűjteménye a Szépművészeti Múzeumban [P.
   Majovszky's Graphic Collection in the Museum of Fine Arts]. "Magyar Művészet" [Hungarian Art],
   1935, p. 148 (illustrated) — Hoffmann, E.: A Majovszky gyűjtemény [Majovszky Collection]. "Európa",
   1943, p. 152 (illustrated) — Tabarant, A.: Manet et ses oeuvres. Paris, 1947, pp. 325—326 (illustrated)
   — Huyghe, R.: Le dessin français au XIXᵉ siècle. Lausanne, 1956, p. 139 (illustrated).

44 RENOIR, FIRMIN-AUGUSTE
  (1841, Limoges — 1919, Cagnes)
   COUNTRY DANCE. 1883.
   Chalk — $19^5/_{16}'' \times 13^9/_{16}''$
   Sketch for a painting formerly in the Durand-Ruel Collection. Resembles a drawing in the César M. de
   Hauke Collection at New York
   The dancers are the painter Lhote and Renoir's future wife
   Signed: "AR"
   Majovszky Coll. — MFA 1935—2761
   Literature: Meller, S.: Handzeichnungen des XIX. Jahrhunderts aus der Sammlung P. v. Majovszky.
   "Die graphischen Künste", 1919, p. 12 (illustrated) — Hausenstein, W.: Renoir. Munich, 1920, Plate
   7 — Rózsaffy, D.: Une exposition de dessins français du XVᵉ au XXᵉ siècle au Musée des Beaux-Arts
   de Budapest. "Le Bulletin de l'Art ancien et moderne", 1933, p. 383 — Meller, S.: Majovszky Pál rajz-
   gyűjteménye a Szépművészeti Múzeumban [P. Majovszky's Graphic Collection in the Museum of Fine
   Arts]. "Magyar Művészet" [Hungarian Art], 1935, p. 137 (illustrated) — Hoffmann, E.: A Majovszky
   gyűjtemény [Majovszky Collection]. "Európa", 1943, p. 154 — Gyergyai, A.: Francia művészet a Szép-
   művészeti Múzeumban [French Art in the Museum of Fine Arts]. "Budapest", 1947, p. 456 (illustrated)
   — Kálmán, M.: Les dessins de Renoir au Musée des Beaux-Arts. "Acta Historiae Artium Academiae
   Scientiarum Hungaricae", Budapest, 1956, Tom. IV, Fasciculus 1—2, p. 104 (illustrated) — Kálmán,
   M.: Renoir rajzai a Szépművészeti Múzeumban [The Drawings of Renoir in the Museum of Fine Arts].
   "Művészettörténeti Értesítő" [Art Historical Bulletin], 1956, p. 18 (illustrated).

45 RENOIR, FIRMIN-AUGUSTE
   BATHERS. 1885.
   Pencil — $14^1/_4'' \times 9^1/_{16}''$
   Sketch for *The Bathers* in the Caroll S. Tyson Collection, Philadelphia
   Majovszky Coll. — MFA 1935—2751
   Literature: Hausenstein, W.: Renoir. Munich, 1920, Plate 9 — Kálmán, M.: Les dessins de Renoir au Musée
   des Beaux-Arts. "Acta Historiae Artium Academiae Scientiarum Hungaricae", Budapest, 1956, Tom.
   IV, Fasciculus 1—2, p. 103 (illustrated) — Kálmán, M.: Renoir rajzai a Szépművészeti Múzeumban [The
   Drawings of Renoir in the Museum of Fine Arts]. "Művészettörténeti Értesítő" [Art Historical Bulletin],
   1956, pp. 16—18 (illustrated).

46 RENOIR, FIRMIN-AUGUSTE
   BOATING PARTY. 1886.
   Watercolor — $11^{15}/_{16}'' \times 18^{11}/_{16}''$
   Signed: "AR"
   Majovszky Coll. — MFA 1935—2762
   Literature: Hausenstein, W.: Renoir. Munich, 1920, Plate 17 — Meller, S.: Majovszky Pál rajzgyűjteménye
   a Szépművészeti Múzeumban [P. Majovszky's Graphic Collection in the Museum of Fine Arts]. "Magyar
   Művészet" [Hungarian Art], 1935, p. 148 (illustrated) — Hoffmann, E.: A Majovszky gyűjtemény [Majov-
   szky Collection]. "Európa", 1943, p. 153 — Kálmán, M.: Les dessins de Renoir au Musée des Beaux-
   Arts. "Acta Historiae Artium Academiae Scientiarum Hungaricae", Budapest, 1956, Tom. IV, Fasciculus
   1—2, p. 117 (illustrated) — Kálmán, M.: Renoir rajzai a Szépművészeti Múzeumban [The Drawings of
   Renoir in the Museum of Fine Arts]. "Művészettörténeti Értesítő" [Art Historical Bulletin], 1956, pp.
   19—21 (illustrated).

47 RENOIR, FIRMIN-AUGUSTE
        BATTLEDORE AND SHUTTLECOCK. 1887.
        Pencil — $12^1/_2$"$\times 10^5/_8$"
        Sketch for the painting in the Minneapolis Institute of Art
        Signed: "AR"
        Majovszky Coll. — MFA 1935—2758
        Literature: Kálmán, M.: Les dessins de Renoir au Musée des Beaux-Arts. "Acta Historiae Artium Aca-
        demiae Scientiarum Hungaricae", Budapest, 1956, Tom. IV, Fasciculus 1—2, p. 118 (illustrated) — Kálmán,
        M.: Renoir rajzai a Szépművészeti Múzeumban [The Drawings of Renoir in the Museum of Fine Arts].
        "Művészettörténeti Értesítő" [Art Historical Bulletin], 1956, pp. 20—22 (illustrated).

48 RENOIR, FIRMIN-AUGUSTE
        SEATED WOMAN. 1887.
        Pencil — $12^{11}/_{16}$"$\times 8^7/_8$"
        Signed: "AR AR."
        Majovszky Coll. — MFA 1935—2760
        Literature: Hausenstein, W.: Renoir. Munich, 1920, Plate 11.

49 RENOIR, FIRMIN-AUGUSTE
        THE BRIDGE AT ARGENTEUIL. 1888.
        Watercolor — $6^{13}/_{16}$"$\times 9^1/_{16}$"
        Sketch for the painting in the Mary Harriman Collection, New York
        Signed: "AR"
        Majovszky Coll. — MFA 1935—2763
        Literature: Kálmán, M.: Les dessins de Renoir au Musée des Beaux-Arts. "Acta Historiae Artium Academiae
        Scientiarum Hungaricae", Budapest, 1956, Tom. IV, Fasciculus 1—2, p. 120 (illustrated) — Kálmán,
        M.: Renoir rajzai a Szépművészeti Múzeumban [The Drawings of Renoir in the Museum of Fine Arts].
        "Művészettörténeti Értesítő" [Art Historical Bulletin], 1956, pp. 20—23 (illustrated).

50 RENOIR, FIRMIN-AUGUSTE
        THE MUSIC LESSON. 1891.
        Chalk — $14^9/_{16}$"$\times 13^1/_{16}$"
        Sketch for the painting formerly in the Durand-Ruel Collection
        Signed: "AR"
        Majovszky Coll. — MFA 1935—2756
        Literature: Hausenstein, W.: Renoir. Munich, 1920, Plate 13 — Hevesy, I.: Az impresszionizmus művé-
        szete [The Art of Impressionism]. Gyoma, 1922, p. 23 (illustrated) — Rózsaffy, D.: Une exposition de
        dessins français du XVe au XXe siècle au Musée des Beaux-Arts de Budapest. "Le Bulletin de l'Art ancien
        et moderne", 1933, p. 383 — Kálmán, M.: Les dessins de Renoir au Musée des Beaux-Arts. "Acta His-
        toriae Artium Academiae Scientiarum Hungaricae", Budapest, 1956, Tom. IV, Fasciculus 1—2, p. 121
        (illustrated) — Kálmán, M.: Renoir rajzai a Szépművészeti Múzeumban [The Drawings of Renoir in the
        Museum of Fine Arts]. "Művészettörténeti Értesítő" [Art Historical Bulletin], 1956, pp. 21—23 (illustrated).

51 RENOIR, FIRMIN-AUGUSTE
        AFTER THE BATH. 1894 (?)
        Chalk — $18^{13}/_{16}$"$\times 12^5/_{16}$"
        Signed : "AR"
        Majovszky Coll. — MFA 1935—2755
        Literature: Hausenstein, W.: Renoir. Munich, 1920, Plate 15 — Meller, S.: Majovszky Pál rajzgyűjteménye
        a Szépművészeti Múzeumban [P. Majovszky's Graphic Collection in the Museum of Fine Arts]. "Magyar
        Művészet" [Hungarian Art], 1935, p. 144 (illustrated) — Hoffmann, E.: A Majovszky gyűjtemény [Ma-
        jovszky Collection]. "Európa", 1943, p. 153.

52 DEGAS, HILAIRE-GERMAIN-EDGAR
    (1834, Paris — 1917, Paris)
        STUDY OF A DANCER DRESSING
        Chalk — $12^3/_4$"$\times 9^7/_{16}$"
        Signed: "Degas"
        Majovszky Coll. — MFA 1935—2689
        Literature: Hevesy, I.: Az impresszionizmus művészete [The Art of Impressionism]. Gyoma, 1922, p. 35
        (illustrated).

53 DEGAS, HILAIRE-GERMAIN-EDGAR
DANCER. 1899.
Pastel — 12″ × 12³/₈″
Study for the pastel in the Toledo (USA) Museum of Art. A motif figuring on numerous drawings and pastels
Signed: "Degas"
Majovszky Coll. — MFA 1935—2690
Literature: Hoffmann, E.: A Majovszky gyűjtemény [Majovszky Collection]. "Európa", 1943, p. 153.

54 PISSARRO, CAMILLE
(1831, Ile-Saint-Thomas — 1903, Paris)
ON A BENCH
Chalk and India ink wash — 14¹⁵/₁₆″ × 7¹/₁₆″
Signed: "C. P."
Donated by S. Meller — MFA 1927—2006.

55 SISLEY, ALFRED
(1839, Paris — 1899, Moret-sur-Loing)
THE CHURCH AT MORET
Pastel — 11¹³/₁₆″ × 9³/₁₆″
Study for the painting in the Petit Palais in Paris
Signed: "Sisley"
Majovszky Coll. — MFA 1935—2787
Literature: Hoffmann, E.: A Majovszky gyűjtemény [Majovszky Collection]. "Európa", 1943, p. 152.

56 SISLEY, ALFRED
EARLY SNOW IN A FRENCH VILLAGE
Pastel — 7³/₁₆″ × 12″
Study for the painting formerly in the National Gallery of Berlin
Signed: "Sisley"
Majovszky Coll. — MFA 1935—2788
Literature: Hoffmann, E.: A Majovszky gyűjtemény [Majovszky Collection]. "Európa", 1943, p. 152.

57 SISLEY, ALFRED
GEESE
Pastel — 7¹³/₁₆″ × 12¹/₈″
Signed: "Sisley"
Majovszky Coll. — MFA 1935—2786
Literature: Hoffmann, E.: A Majovszky gyűjtemény [Majovszky Collection]. "Európa", 1943, p. 152.

58 TOULOUSE-LAUTREC, HENRI DE
(1864, Albi — 1901, Château de Mâlromé)
MLLE. MARCELLE LENDER
Pencil — 13¹/₄″ × 9¹⁵/₁₆″
Majovszky Coll. — MFA 1935—2729.

59 TOULOUSE-LAUTREC, HENRI DE
AT THE MOULIN ROUGE
Chalk and gouache — 22³/₁₆″ × 16¹/₂″
Marked with the artist's monogram
Majovszky Coll. — MFA 1935—2728
Literature: Meller, S.: Majovszky Pál rajzgyűjteménye a Szépművészeti Múzeumban [P. Majovszky's Graphic Collection in the Museum of Fine Arts]. "Magyar Művészet" [Hungarian Art], 1935, p. 152 (illustrated) — Hoffmann, E.: A Majovszky gyűjtemény [Majovszky Collection]. "Európa", 1943, p. 153.

60 FORAIN, JEAN-LOUIS
(1852, Reims — 1931, Paris)
AFTER THE VISION. 1909.
Pencil and sepia wash — 9⁷/₁₆″ × 12⁵/₁₆″
Study for the etching (Guérin 82)
Signed: "forain"
Guérin Coll. — Majovszky Coll. — MFA 1935—2707
Literature: Guérin, M.: J. L. Forain. Paris, 1912, No. 82.

22

61 R O D I N , A U G U S T E
(1840, Paris — 1917, Meudon)
S T U D Y F O R T H E H E A D O F M M E. S É V É R I N E
Chalk — 12⁵/₈″×10⁵/₈″
Signed: "A R"
Majovszky Coll. — MFA 1935—2767
Literature: Meller, S.: Handzeichnungen des XIX. Jahrhunderts aus der Sammlung P. v. Majovszky. "Die graphischen Künste", 1919 (illustrated) — Meller, S.: Majovszky Pál rajzgyűjteménye a Szépművészeti Múzeumban [P. Majovszky's Graphic Collection in the Museum of Fine Arts]. "Magyar Művészet" [Hungarian Art], 1935, p. 149 (illustrated) — Hoffmann, E.: A Majovszky gyűjtemény [Majovszky Collection]. "Európa", 1943, pp. 153—155 (illustrated).

62 R O D I N , A U G U S T E
S T U D Y
Pencil and India ink wash — 6¹⁵/₁₆″×4¹³/₁₆″
Majovszky Coll. — MFA 1935—2774.

63 R O D I N , A U G U S T E
N U D E W O M A N
Pencil and watercolor — 12⁵/₈″×8¹/₄″
Signed: "A Rodin"
Majovszky Coll. — MFA 1935—2777.

64 R O D I N , A U G U S T E
T W O N U D E S
Pencil and watercolor wash — 12¹³/₁₆″×9¹³/₁₆″
Signed: "A Monsieur Hatvany Ferencz Aug. Rodin"
Donated by Ferenc Hatvany — MFA 1920—688.

65 R O D I N , A U G U S T E
N U D E
Pencil and watercolor wash — 12⁵/₈″×9³/₄″
Signed: "A R"
Majovszky Coll. — MFA 1935—2776
Literature: Rózsaffy, D.: Une exposition de dessins français du XVᵉ au XXᵉ siècle au Musée des Beaux-Arts de Budapest. "Le Bulletin de l'Art ancien et moderne", 1933, p. 383.

66 S E U R A T , G E O R G E S - P I E R R E
(1859, Paris — 1891, Paris)
V A G A B O N D
Chalk — 12¹/₄″×8¹/₈″
Signed: "G. Seurat"
Majovszky Coll. — MFA 1935—2784.

67 S I G N A C , P A U L
(1863, Paris — 1935, Paris)
R I V E R B A N K
Watercolor — 8³/₄″×15⁷/₈″
Signed: "P. Signac Samois 1900"
Stern Collection in Berlin — Majovszky Coll. — MFA 1935—2785.

68 C É Z A N N E , P A U L
(1839, Aix en Provence — 1906, Aix en Provence)
S K E T C H E S
Pencil — 8⁷/₁₆″×11¹/₄″
Majovszky Coll. — MFA 1935—2678
Literature: Venturi, L.: Cézanne. Son art, son oeuvre. Paris, 1936, No. 1221 (illustrated).

69 CÉZANNE, PAUL
SELF-PORTRAIT
(On the verso, sketches)
Pencil — 11 $^{13}/_{16}$" × 9 $^{7}/_{8}$"
Majovszky Coll. — MFA 1935—2679
Literature: Meller, S.: Handzeichnungen des XIX. Jahrhunderts aus der Sammlung P. v. Majovszky. "Die graphischen Künste", 1919, p. 14 (illustrated) — Cézanne und seine Ahnen. Thirty-third publication of the Marées Gesellschaft, Munich, 1921, Plate 7 — Lázár, B.: Cézanne. "Magyar Művészet" [Hungarian Art], 1930, p. 623 (illustrated) — Rózsaffy, D.: Une exposition de dessins français du XVe au XXe siècle au Musée des Beaux-Arts de Budapest. "Le Bulletin de l'Art ancien et moderne", 1933, p. 383 — Venturi, L.: Cézanne. Son art, son oeuvre. Paris, 1936, No. 1237 (illustrated) — Hoffmann, E.: A Majovszky gyűjtemény [Majovszky Collection]. "Európa", 1943, pp. 153—156 (illustrated) — Gyergyai, A.: Francia művészet a Szépművészeti Múzeumban [French Art in the Museum of Fine Arts]. "Budapest", 1947, p. 452 (illustrated) — Huyghe, R.: Le dessin français au XIXe siècle. Lausanne, 1956, p. 100 (illustrated).

70 CÉZANNE, PAUL
FRUIT STILL LIFE
Watercolor — 9 $^{3}/_{8}$" × 12 $^{1}/_{2}$"
Majovszky Coll. — MFA 1935—2677
Literature: Lázár, B.: Cézanne. "Magyar Művészet" [Hungarian Art], 1930, p. 631 (illustrated) — Venturi, L.: Cézanne. Son art, son oeuvre. Paris, 1936, No. 858 (illustrated) — Hoffmann, E.: A Majovszky gyűjtemény [Majovszky Collection]. "Európa", 1943, p. 153 — Huyghe, R.: Le dessin français au XIXe siècle. Lausanne, 1956, p. 98 (illustrated).

71 CÉZANNE, PAUL
PLASTER FIGURE OF CUPID. c. 1885.
Pencil and watercolor — 18 $^{7}/_{8}$" × 12 $^{3}/_{8}$"
The statue may be seen in several paintings (in the Gagnat and Courtauld Collections, Paris) and watercolors of Cézanne's
Majovszky Coll. — MFA 1935—2676
Literature: Meller, S.: Handzeichnungen des XIX. Jahrhunderts aus der Sammlung P. v. Majovszky. "Die graphischen Künste", 1919, p. 15 (illustrated) — Cézanne und seine Ahnen. Thirty-third publication of the Marées Gesellschaft, Munich, 1921, Plate 21 — Lázár, B.: Cézanne. "Magyar Művészet" [Hungarian Art], 1930, p. 632 (illustrated) — Rózsaffy, D.: Une exposition de dessins français du XVe au XXe siècle au Musée des Beaux-Arts de Budapest. "Le Bulletin de l'Art ancien et moderne", 1933, p. 383 — Venturi, L.: Cézanne. Son art, son oeuvre. Paris, 1936, No. 1083 (illustrated) — Hoffmann, E.: A Majovszky gyűjtemény [Majovszky Collection]. "Európa", 1943, pp. 150—153 (illustrated).

72 CÉZANNE, PAUL
LANDSCAPE
Watercolor — 12 $^{5}/_{16}$" × 18 $^{13}/_{16}$"
Majovszky Coll. — MFA 1935—2675
Literature: Venturi, L.: Cézanne. Son art, son oeuvre. Paris, 1936, No. 962 (illustrated).

73 PUVIS DE CHAVANNES, PIERRE
(1824, Lyon — 1898, Paris)
SKETCH FOR THE MURAL "GREEK COLONY"
IN THE PALAIS DE LONGCHAMP, MARSEILLE. 1869.
Black and blue chalk — 6 $^{1}/_{8}$" × 7 $^{7}/_{8}$"
Marked with the stamp of the artist's estate
Donated by S. Meller — MFA 1927—2009.

74 GAUGUIN, PAUL
(1848, Paris — 1903, Marquesas Islands)
TAHITIAN SCENE
Watercolor covered with tissue paper — 9 $^{13}/_{16}$" × 12 $^{3}/_{4}$"
Majovszky Coll. — MFA 1935—2716.

75 GAUGUIN, PAUL
TAHITIAN WOMAN
Watercolor and white body color — 6 $^{3}/_{8}$" × 6 $^{13}/_{16}$"
Majovszky Coll. — MFA 1935—2715.

76 B O N N A R D, P I E R R E
   (1867, Fontenay-aux-Roses — 1947, Le Cannet)
        S E L F - P O R T R A I T
        India ink — $6'' \times 6^1/_8''$
        Signed: "PBonnard"
        Majovszky Coll. — MFA 1935—2661
        Literature: Hevesy, I.: A posztimpresszionizmus művészete [The Art of Post-Impressionism]. Gyoma, 1922, p. 93 (illustrated) — Meller, S.: Majovszky Pál rajzgyűjteménye a Szépművészeti Múzeumban [P. Majovszky's Graphic Collection in the Museum of Fine Arts]. "Magyar Művészet" [Hungarian Art], 1935 (illustrated on the cover of No. 5).

77 B O N N A R D, P I E R R E
        T H E Y E L L O W L A M P
        Pencil and watercolor — $7^{15}/_{16}'' \times 6^1/_{16}''$
        Signed: "PBonnard"
        Majovszky Coll. — MFA 1935—2660.

78 B O N N A R D, P I E R R E
        S T U D I E S
        India ink — $12^5/_{16}'' \times 7^3/_4''$
        Signed: "PBonnard"
        Majovszky Coll. — MFA 1935—2663.

79 B O N N A R D, P I E R R E
        T O I L E T T E
        Chalk — $12^5/_{16}'' \times 7^3/_4''$
        Signed: "PBonnard"
        Majovszky Coll. — MFA 1935—2662.

80 M A I L L O L, A R I S T I D E
   (1861, Banyuls-sur-Mer — 1944, Banyuls-sur-Mer)
        S T U D I E S
        Red chalk — $9'' \times 5^{11}/_{16}''$
        Signed: "M"
        Majovszky Coll. — MFA 1935—2732.

81 P I C A S S O, P A B L O
   (1881, Malaga)
        M O T H E R A N D C H I L D. 1904.
        India ink and watercolor — $13^7/_8'' \times 10''$
        A sketch of this composition is in the Fogg Art Museum, Harvard University
        Signed: "Picasso"
        Donated by Ferenc Hatvany — MFA 1918—461
        Literature: Rózsaffy, D.: Une exposition de dessins français du XVe au XXe siècle au Musée des Beaux-Arts de Budapest. "Le Bulletin de l'Art ancien et moderne", 1933, p. 383 — Hajós, E.: Francia rajzok kiállítása a Szépművészeti Múzeumban [Exposition of French Drawings in the Museum of Fine Arts]. "Magyar Művészet" [Hungarian Art], 1933, p. 331 (illustrated).

THE NETHERLANDS

82 J O N G K I N D, J O H A N B A R T H O L D
   (1819, Lattrop — 1891, Côte-Saint-André)
        S E A S I D E
        Chalk and sepia wash — $7^3/_8'' \times 11^{15}/_{16}''$
        Signed: "Jongkind 12 Sept 62"
        Majovszky Coll. — MFA 1935—2794.

83 J O N G K I N D, J O H A N B A R T H O L D
        D U T C H H A R B O R
        Pencil and watercolor — $10^9/_{16}'' \times 17^1/_2''$
        Signed: "Jongkind 1864"
        Majovszky Coll. — 1935—2795.

84 G O G H, V I N C E N T V A N
(1853, Groot-Zundert — 1890, Auvers-sur-Oise)
W O R K I N G W O M A N
Charcoal — 12 $^7/_8$″ × 10 $^3/_8$″
Majovszky Coll. — MFA 1935—2793
Literature: Vollard, A.: Lettres de Vincent van Gogh à E. Bernard. Paris, 1911, Plate 31 — Meller, S.:
Handzeichnungen des XIX. Jahrhunderts aus der Sammlung P. v. Majovszky. "Die graphischen Künste",
1919, p. 31 (illustrated) — Éber, L.: Van Gogh tragikuma [The Element of Tragedy in Van Gogh]. "Ars
Una", 1923, p. 21 (illustrated) — Faille, J. B. de la: L'oeuvre de Vincent van Gogh. III, 1928, No. 1204.
(The reference is erroneous, the drawing on plate 95 is not the one in the Museum of Fine Arts.) — Meller,
S.: Majovszky Pál rajzgyűjteménye a Szépművészeti Múzeumban [P. Majovszky's Graphic Collection
in the Museum of Fine Arts]. "Magyar Művészet" [Hungarian Art], 1935, p. 145 (illustrated) — Hoffmann,
E.: A Majovszky gyűjtemény [Collection Majovszky]. "Európa", 1943, p. 154.

85 G O G H, V I N C E N T V A N
T H E G A R D E N O F N U E N E N I N W I N T E R
Pen and bister, and white body color — 20 $^1/_4$″ × 15″
Resembles a drawing in the Van Gogh Collection at Amsterdam
Signed: "Vincent"
Majovszky Coll. — MFA 1935—2791
Literature: Vollard, A.: Lettres de Vincent van Gogh à E. Bernard. Paris, 1911, Plate 32 — Meller, S.:
Handzeichnungen des XIX. Jahrhunderts aus der Sammlung P. v. Majovszky. "Die graphischen Künste",
1919 (illustrated) — Éber, L.: Van Gogh tragikuma [The Element of Tragedy in Van Gogh]. "Ars Una",
1923, p. 23 — Faille, J. B. de la: L'oeuvre de Vincent van Gogh. III, 1928, No. 1130, Plate 74 — Hajós,
E. M.: Budapester Privatsammlungen. "Der Kunstwanderer", 1932, p. 219 (illustrated) — Meller, S.:
Majovszky Pál rajzgyűjteménye a Szépművészeti Múzeumban [P. Majovszky's Graphic Collection in the
Museum of Fine Arts]. "Magyar Művészet" [Hungarian Art], 1935, p. 143 (illustrated) — Hoffmann E.:
A Majovszky gyűjtemény [Majovszky Collection]. "Európa", 1943, p. 154.

86 G O G H, V I N C E N T V A N
H A Y S T A C K S I N P R O V E N C E. A R L E S 1888.
Pen and India ink — 9 $^1/_2$″ × 12 $^9/_{16}$″
A similar drawing owned by Pierre Matisse, New York. A painting almost identical with the drawing
in the Kröller-Müller Collection, Otterlo
Majovszky Coll. — MFA 1935—2792
Literature: Vollard, A.: Lettres de Vincent van Gogh à E. Bernard. Paris, 1911, Plate 59 — Hevesy, I.:
A posztimpresszionizmus művészete [The Art of Post-Impressionism]. Gyoma, 1922, p. 41 (illustrated)
— Éber, L.: Van Gogh tragikuma [The Element of Tragedy in Van Gogh]. "Ars Una", 1923, p. 25 —
Faille, J. B. de la: L'oeuvre de Vincent van Gogh, III, 1928, No. 1426, Plate 151 — Hoffmann, E.: A Majov-
szky gyűjtemény [Majovszky Collection]. "Európa", 1943, p. 154.

AUSTRIA AND GERMANY

87 K R I E H U B E R, J O S E P H
(1800, Vienna — 1876, Vienna)
T H E C H I L D R E N O F C O U N T K A J E T Á N E R D Ő D Y
Watercolor and white body color — 19 $^7/_8$″ × 16 $^1/_4$″
Signed: "Kriehuber 839"
MFA 1950—4239.

88 A L T, R U D O L F V O N
(1812, Vienna — 1905, Vienna)
T H E O L D N A T I O N A L T H E A T E R I N B U D A P E S T
(On the verso, a pen drawing)
Pencil and watercolor — 7″ × 9 $^{11}/_{16}$″
Sketch for plate 15 of the series Malerische Ansichten von Ofen und Pest, lithographed by F. J. Sandmann
MFA 1937—3078
Literature: Hevesi, L.: R. Alt. Vienna, 1911, pp. 97 and 167 (illustrated).

89 A L T, R U D O L F V O N
T H E N A T I O N A L M U S E U M I N B U D A P E S T
Watercolor — 7″ × 10″
Sketch for plate 16 of the series Malerische Ansichten von Ofen und Pest, lithographed by F. J. Sandmann
MFA 1951—4523.

90 MENZEL, ADOLPH VON
(1815, Breslau — 1905, Berlin)
CHURCH INTERIOR
Pencil — 12$^{13}/_{16}$″×9$^{7}/_{16}$″
Signed: "A. M. 18 Aug. 83"
Majovszky Coll. — MFA 1935—2870
Literature: Meller, S.: Handzeichnungen des XIX. Jahrhunderts aus der Sammlung P. v. Majovszky.
"Die graphischen Künste", 1919, p. 25 (illustrated) — Meller, S.: Majovszky Pál rajzgyűjteménye a Szép-
művészeti Múzeumban [P. Majovszky's Graphic Collection in the Museum of Fine Arts]. "Magyar
Művészet" [Hungarian Art], 1935, p. 150 (illustrated) — Hoffmann, E.: A Majovszky gyűjtemény [Ma-
jovszky Collection]. "Európa", 1943, p. 154.

91 MARÉES, HANS VON
(1837, Elberfeld — 1887, Rome)
SKETCH FOR THE COMPOSITION "IDYLLS". 1873—74.
(Also on the verso)
Pencil — 20$^{9}/_{16}$″×16$^{3}/_{8}$″
Balling Coll. — Majovszky Coll. — MFA 1935—2866
Literature: Meier-Graefe, J.: H. v. Marées. Munich—Leipzig, 1909, Nos. 232 and 232/a — Meller, S.:
Handzeichnungen des XIX. Jahrhunderts aus der Sammlung P. v. Majovszky. "Die graphischen Künste",
1919 (illustrated) — Meller, S.: Majovszky Pál rajzgyűjteménye a Szépművészeti Múzeumban [P. Majov-
szky's Graphic Collection in the Museum of Fine Arts]. "Magyar Művészet" [Hungarian Art], 1935, p.
151 (illustrated) — Hoffmann, E.: A Majovszky gyűjtemény [Majovszky Collection]. "Európa", 1943,
p. 155.

92 LIEBERMANN, MAX
(1847, Berlin — 1935, Berlin)
PORTRAIT OF WILHELM VON BODE. 1904.
Chalk — 10$^{3}/_{16}$″×6$^{7}/_{8}$″
Study for the painting in the State Museum of Berlin
Majovszky Coll. — MFA 1935—2861
Literature: "Magyar Művészet" [Hungarian Art], 1929, p. 177 (illustrated) — Hoffmann, E.: A Majovszky
gyűjtemény [Majovszky Collection]. "Európa", 1943, p. 156.

93 LIEBERMANN, MAX
SELF-PORTRAIT. 1908.
Chalk — 13$^{9}/_{16}$″×11$^{7}/_{16}$″
Majovszky Coll. — MFA 1935—2862
Literature: Meller, S.: Handzeichnungen des XIX. Jahrhunderts aus der Sammlung P. v. Majovszky.
"Die graphischen Künste", 1919, p. 28 (illustrated).

94 KOLLWITZ, KÄTHE
(1867, Königsberg — 1945, Moritzburg)
STUDY FOR THE LITHOGRAPHED POSTER OF THE BERLIN
EXPOSITION OF "HEIMARBEIT". 1906.
Pencil and chalk — 15$^{1}/_{4}$″×11$^{1}/_{2}$″
Signed: "Kollwitz"
MFA 1909—2425
Literature: Hajós, E.: Német rajzok kiállítása a Szépművészeti Múzeumban [Exposition of German Draw-
ings in the Museum of Fine Arts]. "Magyar Művészet" [Hungarian Art], 1932, p. 282 (illustrated).

REPRODUCTIONS

5 SIR EDWARD BURNE-JONES

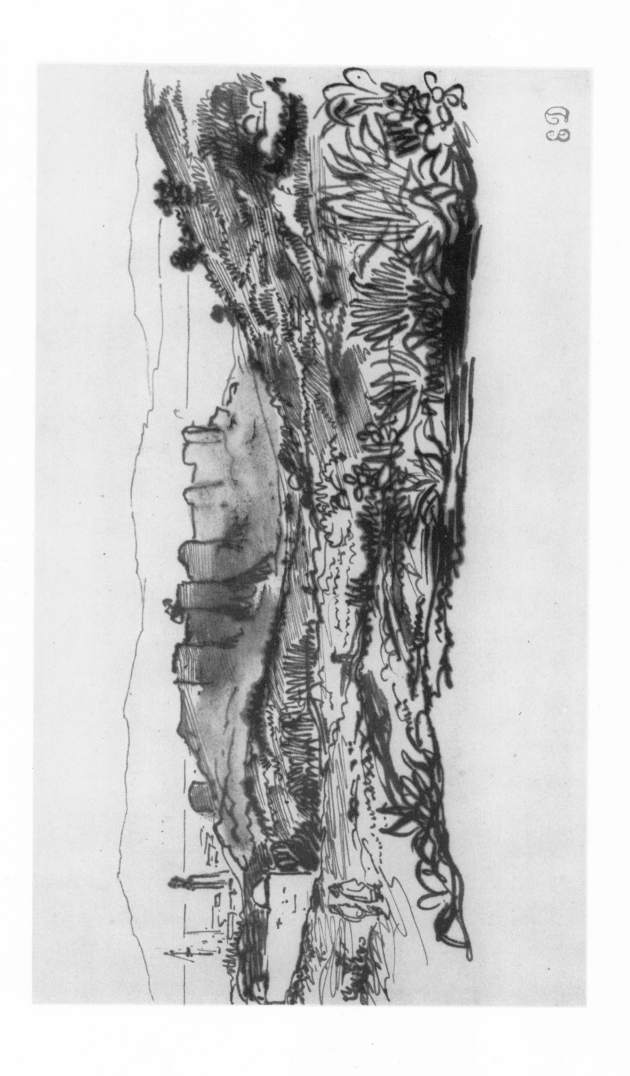

10 EUGÈNE DELACROIX

ECCE

13 GUSTAVE DORÉ

Lasciate ogni speranza voi ch'intrate.

17 CHARLES-FRANÇOIS DAUBIGNY

19 JEAN-BAPTISTE-CAMILLE COROT

J.F.M.

23 JEAN-FRANÇOIS MILLET

25 JEAN-FRANÇOIS MILLET

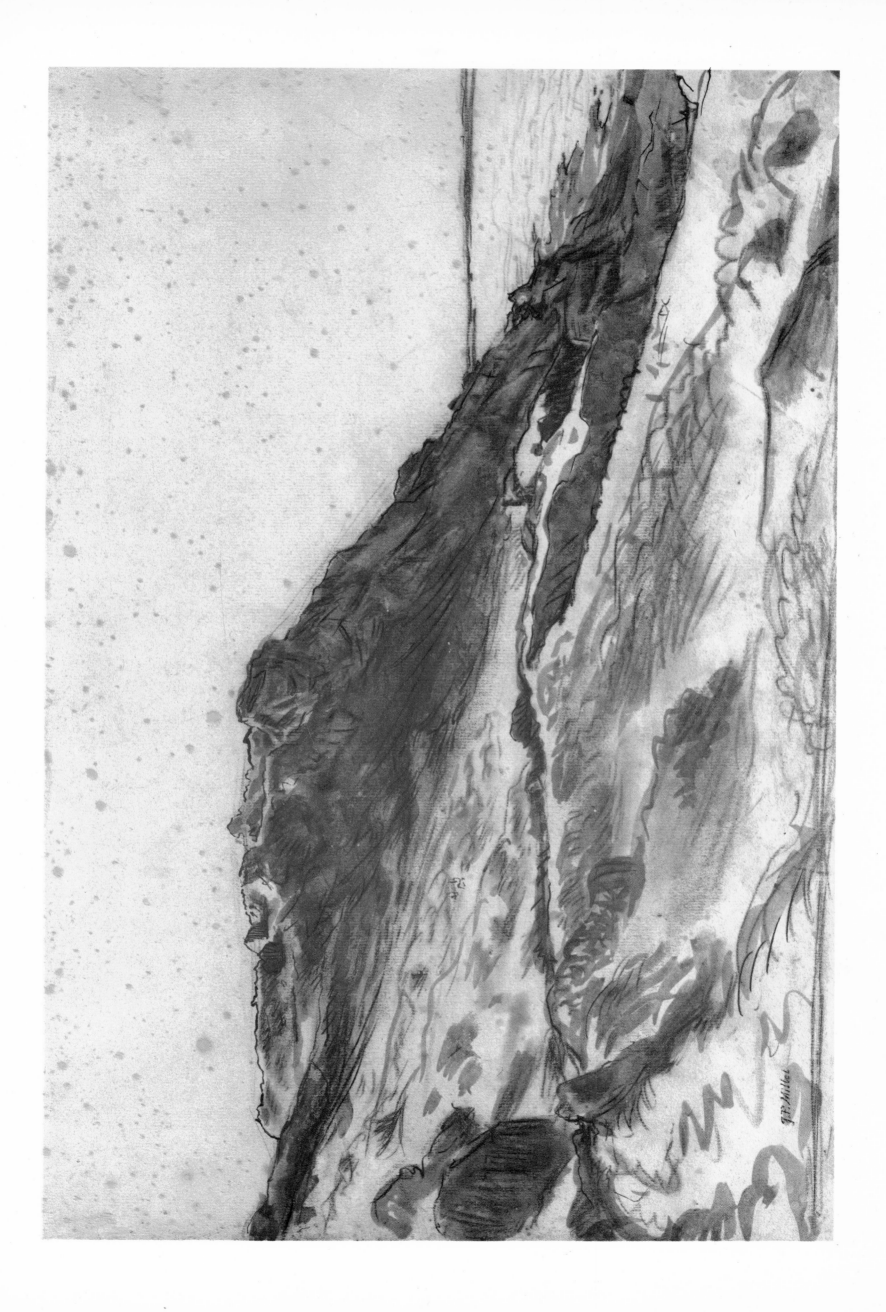

26 HONORÉ DAUMIER

27 HONORÉ DAUMIER

29 HONORÉ DAUMIER

31 CONSTANTIN GUYS

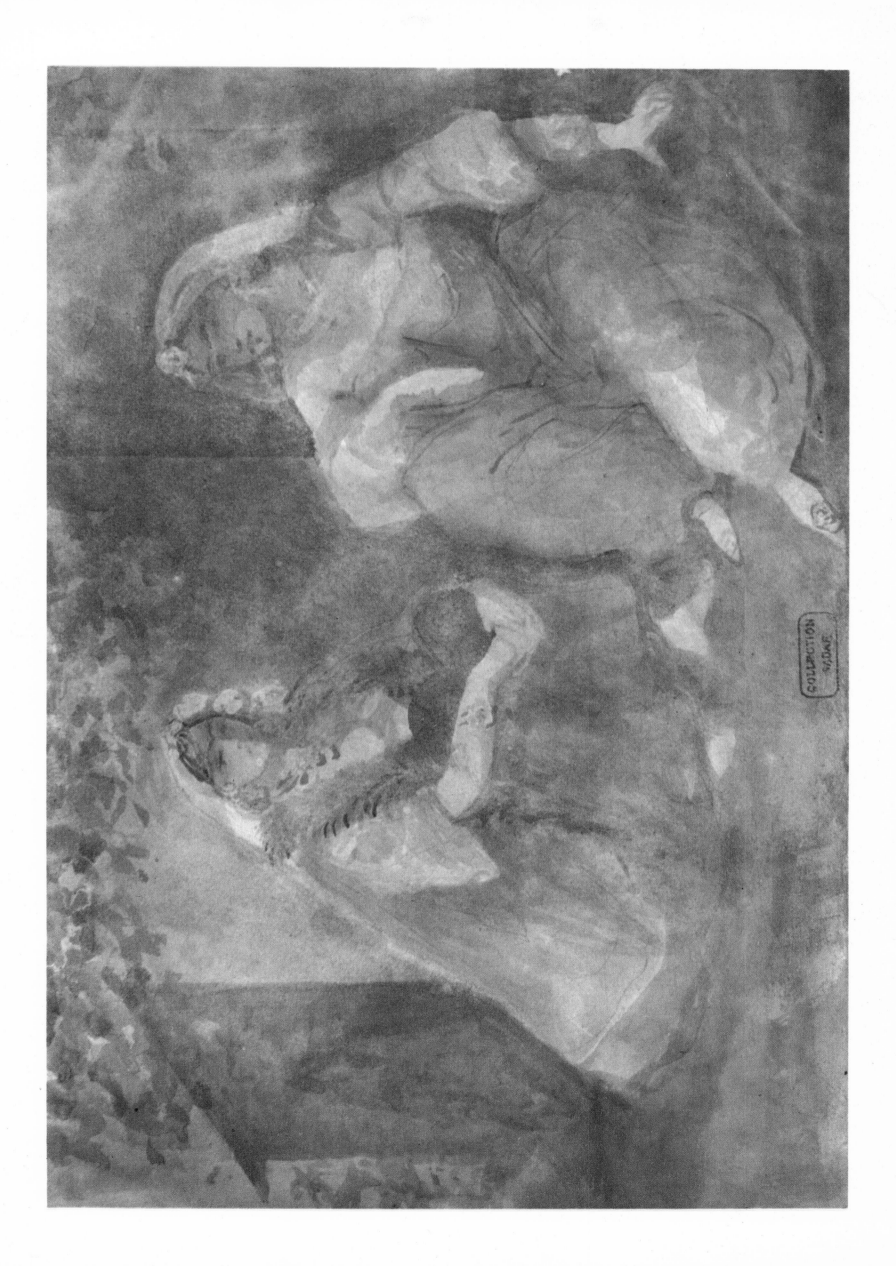

QUARTIER GÉNÉRAL.

3e Secteur.

17, Rue de l'Argonne.

45 FIRMIN-AUGUSTE RENOIR

46 FIRMIN-AUGUSTE RENOIR

49 FIRMIN-AUGUSTE RENOIR

Soigner
les bracelets

très blanche de peau
un peu verdâtre

Degas

53 HILAIRE-GERMAIN-EDGAR DEGAS

54 CAMILLE PISSARRO

56 ALFRED SISLEY

59 HENRI DE TOULOUSE-LAUTREC

61 AUGUSTE RODIN

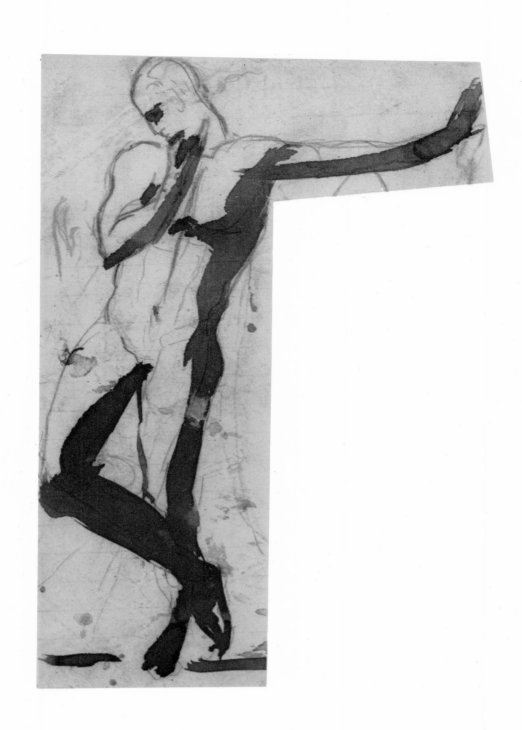

63 AUGUSTE RODIN

À monsieur Hatvany Ferencz
Ing. Rodin

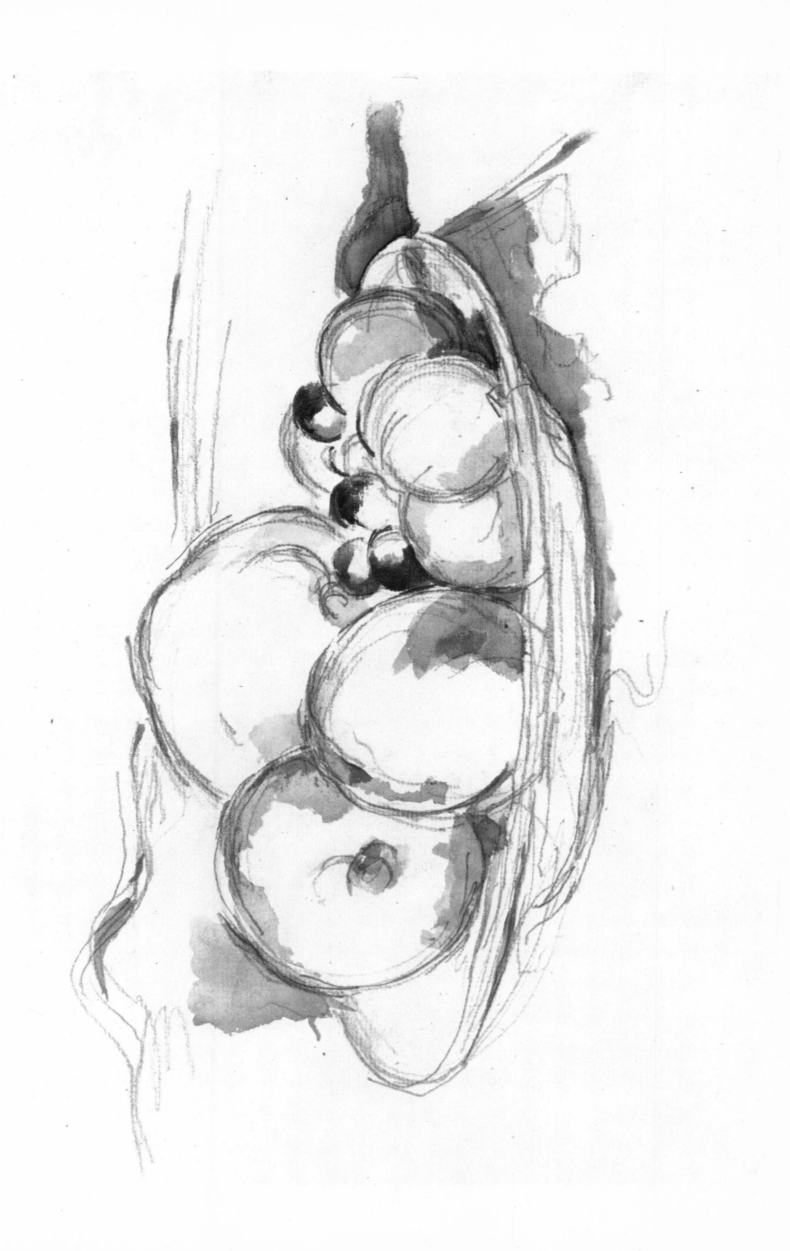

71 PAUL CÉZANNE

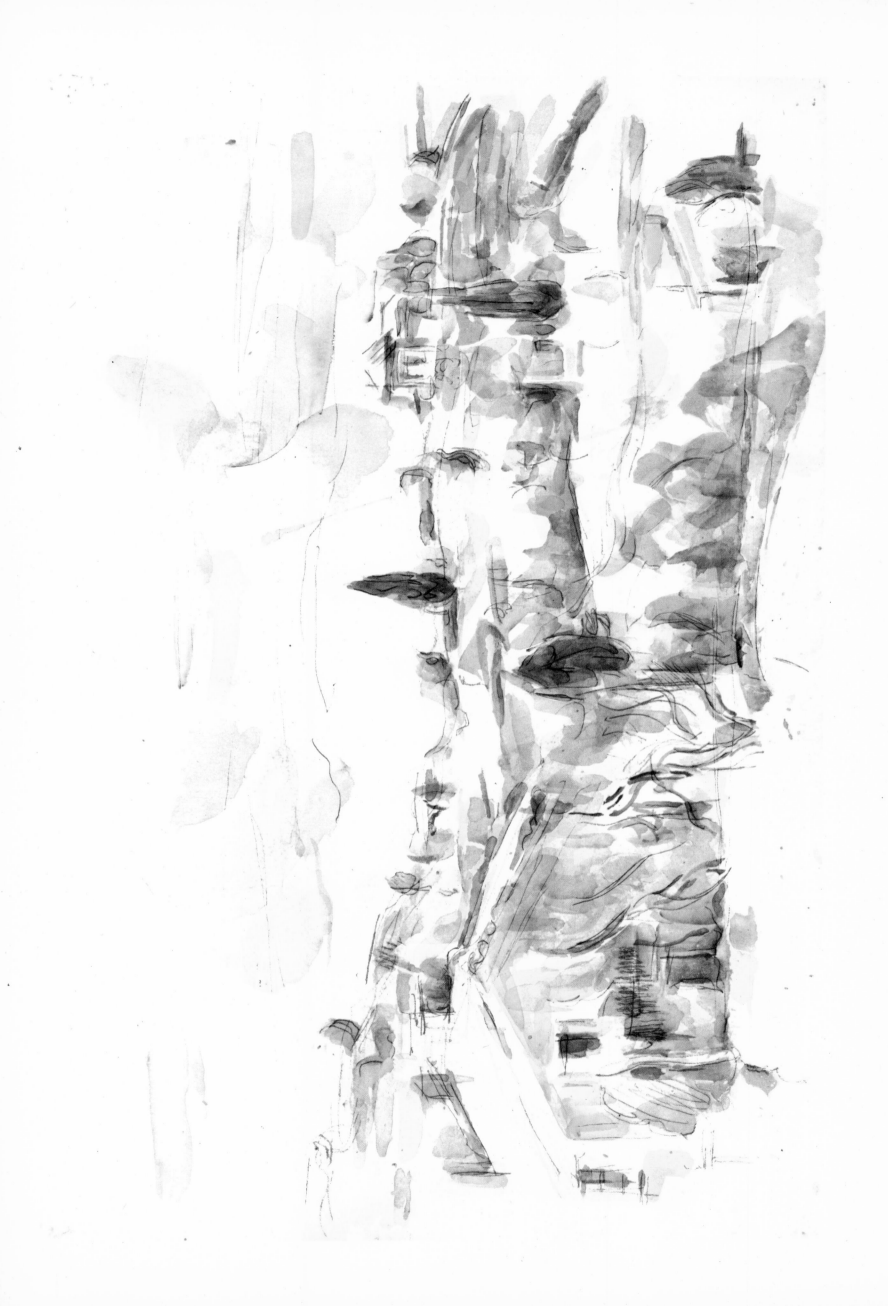

75 PAUL GAUGUIN

77 PIERRE BONNARD

81 PABLO PICASSO

84 VINCENT VAN GOGH

85 VINCENT VAN GOGH

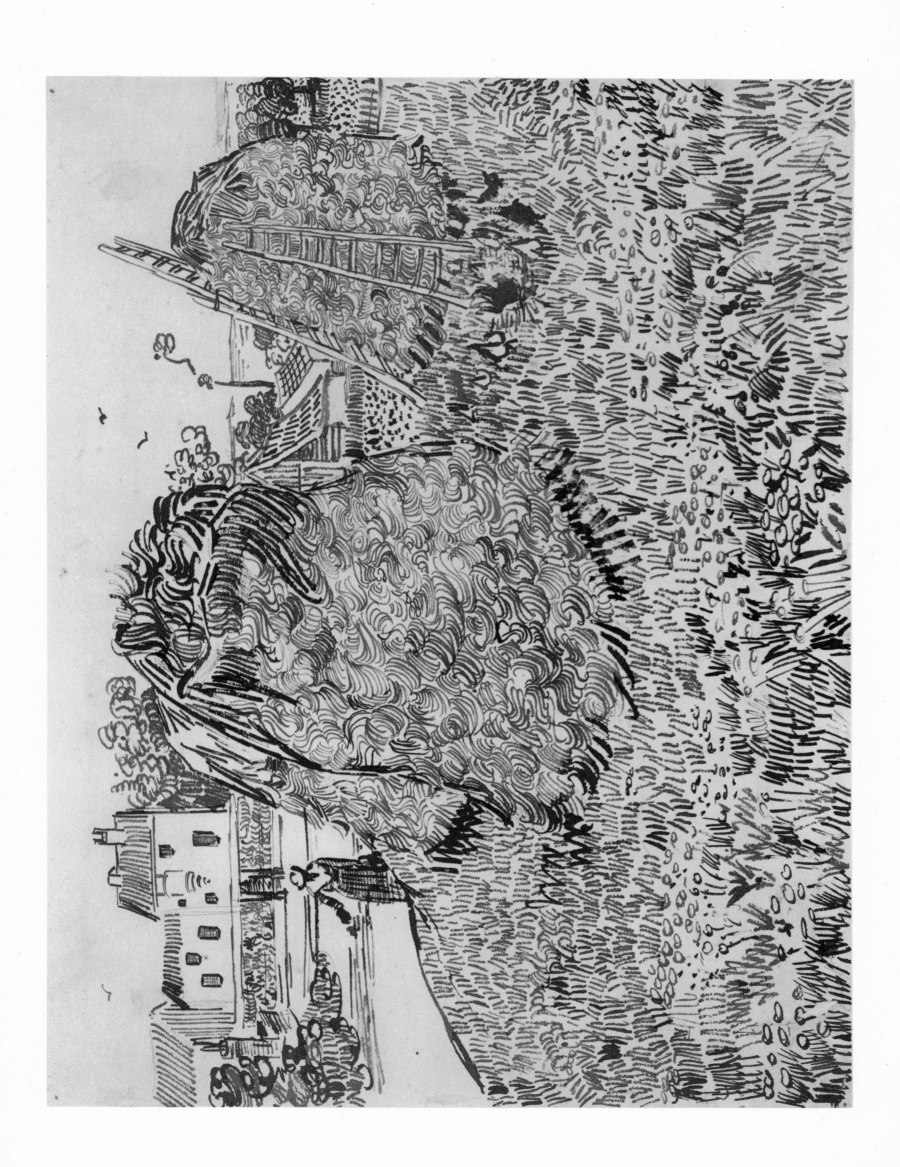

88 RUDOLF VON ALT

94 KÄTHE KOLLWITZ